Great Quotes from Great Sports Heroes

Compiled by Peggy Anderson

Illustrated by Rick Gonnella

CAREER PRESS
3 Tice Road, P.O. Box 687
Franklin Lakes, NJ 07417
1-800-CAREER-1
201-848-0310 (NJ and outside U.S.)
FAX: 201-848-1727

Copyright © 1997 by The Career Press, Inc.

All rights reserved under the Pan-American and International Copyright Conventions. This book may not be reproduced, in whole or in part, in any form or by any means electronic or mechanical, including photocopying, recording, or by any information storage and retrieval system now known or hereafter invented, without written permission from the publisher, The Career Press.

SUCCESSORIES: GREAT QUOTES FROM GREAT SPORTS HEROES

Cover design by The Hub Graphics Corp.

Printed in the U.S.A. by Book-mart Press

To order this title, please call toll-free 1-800-CAREER-1 (NJ and Canada: 201-848-0310) to order using VISA or MasterCard, or for further information on books from Career Press.

Library of Congress Cataloging-in-Publication Data

Great quotes from great sports heroes.
     p.   cm. -- (Successories)
  Rev. ed. of: Great American sports heroes. 1994.
  ISBN 1-56414-287-6 (pbk.)
  1. Sports--Quotations, maxims, etc. 2. Athletes--Quotations.
I. Great American sports heroes. II. Series.
GV706.8.G728 1997
796'.02--dc21   96-51724
                                           CIP

This book is dedicated with love to my stepfather, Richard Crisorio.

Chris Evert

1954 -

The consistency of her performance and her steady baseline play made Chris Evert one of the most successful women in professional tennis. She won at least one major singles championship every year for 13 consecutive years, a record. An exemplary professional in her relations with her colleagues, the press and the public, she was the first player to win 1,000 singles matches as well as 150 tournaments, and the first woman to earn $1 million in prize money. Her winning percentage, .8996, is the highest in the history of professional tennis.

"If you can react the same way to winning and losing, that's a big accomplishment. That quality is important because it stays with you the rest of your life, and there's going to be a life after tennis that's a lot longer than your tennis life."

"Ninety percent of my game is mental. It's my concentration that has gotten me this far."

"Every time, all the time, I'm a perfectionist. I feel I should never lose."

Henry Aaron
Major league outfielder

"I don't want them to forget Ruth. I just want them to remember me!"

Annie Dillard
Writer

"A baseball weighted your hand just so, and fit it. Its red stitches, its good leather and hardness like skin over bone, seemed to call forth a skill both easy and precise."

Bobby Locke
PGA golfer

"Drive for show. But putt for dough."

Earl Campbell
NFL fullback

"Somebody will always break your records. It is how you live that counts."

Philip K. Wrigley
Owner, Chicago Cubs

"Baseball is too much of a sport to be called a business, and too much of a business to be called a sport."

Samuel Johnson
Essayist, writer

"Golf—a game in which you claim the privileges of age and retain the playthings of childhood."

Billie Jean King
1943 -

When Billie Jean King soundly defeated the self-proclaimed male chauvinist Bobby Riggs in an exhibition tennis match televised around the world, she bolstered the cause of women's rights and ignited public interest in championship tennis.

A graceful stylist on the court, King was the singles champion at Wimbledon on six separate occasions. She was the U.S. champion four times and, with her victory at the Virginia Slims-Thunderbird tournament at Phoenix, she became the first woman professional, and the first woman athlete in history, to earn $100,000 during a single competitive year.

"[Tennis is] a perfect combination of violent action taking place in an atmosphere of total tranquillity."

"A champion is afraid of losing. Everyone else is afraid of winning."

"Certain people helping in certain sports. Certain sports are made for certain people—every athlete must find the sport for which he or she is best suited."

Joe Frazier
Heavyweight boxer

"Kill the body and the head will die."

Mike Singletary
NFL linebacker

"Do you know what my favorite part of the game is? The opportunity to play. It is as simple as that. God, I love that opportunity."

Satchel Paige
Major league pitcher

"I never threw an illegal pitch. The trouble is, once in a while I toss one that ain't never been seen by this generation."

Frank Gifford
NFL halfback

"Pro football is like nuclear warfare. There are no winners, only survivors."

John F. Kennedy
35th president of the United States

"We are inclined to think that if we watch a football game or a baseball game, we have taken part in it."

Don Marquis
Writer

"Fishing is a delusion entirely surrounded by liars in old clothes."

Arthur Ashe

1943 - 1993

A man of enormous character and courage, Arthur Ashe established a record in 1968 that may never be equaled in the world of tennis, winning both the Amateur and U.S. Open championships. With a commanding serve-and-volley game, he became a dominating presence on the courts. For 12 years he was in the World Top Ten, and for 14 years he was in the U.S. Top Ten. He was the first black man to win a U.S. championship and Wimbledon, and the first U.S. tennis player to earn $100,000 in a single season. Ashe wrote a comprehensive book on black sports history, *Hard Road to Glory*, and played a dominant role in the resurgence of the American Davis Cup, both as a player and as team captain.

"Sports and politics do mix. Behind the scenes, the two are as inextricably interwoven as any two issues can be."

"One important key to success is self-confidence. An important key to self-confidence is preparation."

"If it had not been for the wind in my face, I wouldn't be able to fly at all."

Edna Ferber
Writer

"Any man who can look handsome in a dirty baseball suit is an Adonis."

Paul Westphal
NBA guard, coach

"The key to any game is to use your strengths and hide your weaknesses."

Bob Plager
NHL coach

"Coaching that team is like having a window seat on the Hindenberg."
[Reflecting on the Toronto Maple Leafs.]

Frank Layden
NBA coach

"When I was coaching, the one thought that I would try to get across to my players was that everything I do each day, everything I say, I must first think what effect it will have on everyone concerned."

Cotton Fitzsimmons
NBA coach

"I have a basic philosophy that I've tried to follow during my coaching career. Whether you're winning or losing, it is important to always be yourself. You can't change because of the circumstances around you."

Babe Ruth

1895 - 1948

Decades after his final appearance at home plate, the name of Babe Ruth is still spoken with admiration and affection. He is the stuff of legends, baseball's quintessential slugger. Until the time of Hank Aaron, Ruth's accomplishments seemed unapproachable—714 home runs and 2,211 runs batted in. And though he ranks second to Aaron in the record books in both categories today, he hit more home runs more often than any other man. He averaged one home run for every 11.76 at-bats, compared to Aaron who managed only one home run every 16.38 trips to the plate. Ruth also remains the leader in slugging percentage, at .690—once posting an .847 single-season slugging percentage, the highest ever—and bases on balls, at 2,056. More importantly, when people speak of accomplishments of epic proportions in any life endeavor, they inevitably mention Babe Ruth.

"You just can't beat the person who never gives up."

"A part of control is learning to correct your weaknesses."

"The way a team plays as a whole determines its success."

Earvin "Magic" Johnson
NBA guard

"Even when I went to the playground, I never picked the best players. I picked guys with less talent, but who were willing to work hard, who had the desire to be great."

Roger Staubach
NFL quarterback, sports broadcaster

"Nothing good comes in life or athletics unless a lot of hard work has preceded the effort. Only temporary success is achieved by taking short cuts."

Roger Maris
Major league outfielder

"You hit home runs not by chance, but by preparation."

Jack Lemmon
Actor

"If you think it's hard to meet new people, try picking up the wrong golf ball."

Sir Edmund Hillary
Mountain climber

"You don't have to be a fantastic hero to do certain things—to compete. You can be just an ordinary chap, sufficiently motivated to reach challenging goals."

Ted Williams

1918 -

Often ignored by the press during his remarkable career, today Ted Williams stands as one of the finest hitters to ever play the game of baseball. He missed three years during his prime serving in World War II and another two seasons during the Korean War, yet still managed to complete his career with a .344 lifetime batting average, 521 home runs and a .634 slugging percentage. His concentration at the plate was legendary, his batting eye unerring. As proof of his abilities, in 1957, at the age of 39, he batted .388 to lead the league, and hit 38 home runs. The next year, his .328 average led the league again. In all, he captured six batting titles, four home run championships, led the American League in slugging percentage nine different times and captured two Triple Crowns.

"I'd rather swing a bat than do anything else in the world."

"All I want out of life is that when I walk down the street, folks will say, 'There goes the greatest hitter who ever lived.'"

Roger Kahn
Writer

"You may glory in a team triumphant, but you fall in love with a team in defeat."

John Madden
NFL coach, sports broadcaster

"The only yardstick for success our society has is being a champion. No one remembers anything else."

Ty Cobb
Major league outfielder

"I had to be first all the time—first in everything. All I ever thought about was winning."

Terry Bradshaw
NFL quarterback, sports broadcaster

"When you've got something to prove, there's nothing greater than a challenge."

Bruce Jenner
Decathlete, Olympic gold medalist

"What does a fellow compete for anyway? A gold medal? Money? Glory? No, it's fulfillment."

Henry Aaron
Major league outfielder

"Girls excel at basketball, golf and tennis, and there is no logical reason they shouldn't play baseball."

A. J. Foyt
Race car driver

"You get out in front—you stay out in front."

John Lowenstein
Major league outfielder

"They should move first base back a step to eliminate all the close plays."

Will Rogers
Humorist

"The income tax has made liars out of more Americans than golf."

Marriane Moore
Writer

"Fanaticism? No. Writing is exciting and baseball is like writing."

Lou Holtz
Football coach, University of Notre Dame

"The man who complains about the way the ball bounces is likely the one who dropped it."

Ken Loeffler
NCAA basketball coach, La Salle

"There are only two kinds of coaches—those who have been fired, and those who will be fired."

Earl Campbell
NFL fullback

"If it weren't for the dark days, we wouldn't know what it is to walk in the light."

Larry Bird

1956 -

His command of the court was so complete his teammates never ceased to marvel at the creativity he displayed season after season—but most especially during the pressure-packed play-offs. When Larry Bird arrived in the National Basketball Association in 1979, the Boston Celtics were one of the worst teams in basketball. By 1981 they were the best—beating the Houston Rockets for the NBA Championship. Bird led the Celtics to titles in 1984 and 1986 as well. Individually, he gathered three consecutive Most Valuable Player awards—from 1984 through 1986, only the third player in NBA history to be so honored—was voted play-off MVP twice, and led the U.S. Olympic Dream Team to gold in 1992.

"I really don't like talking about money. All I can say is that the Good Lord must have wanted me to have it."

27

"I always know what's happening on the court. I see a situation occur, and I respond."

"Push yourself again and again. Don't give an inch until the final buzzer sounds."

Jack Hurley
Boxing promoter

"Looking at a fighter who can't punch is like kissing your brother-in-law."

Nadia Comaneci
Gymnast, Olympic gold medalist

"Hard work has made it easy. That is my secret. That is why I win."

Steffi Graf
Champion tennis player

"As long as I can focus on enjoying what I'm doing, having fun, I know I'll play well."

Pete Rose
Major league outfielder, manager

"I'd go through hell in a gasoline suit to play baseball."

Woody Hayes
Football coach, Ohio State

"Anyone who will tear down sports will tear down America. Sports and religion have made America what it is today."

Casey Stengel
Major league manager

"Good pitching will always stop good hitting, and vice versa."

Mike Ditka

1939 -

According to some experts he was the perfect football player—an unparalleled blocker, a driving runner and a sure-handed receiver. Rookie of the Year in 1961, he led the Chicago Bears to their first NFL title in 17 years, making game-winning catches throughout a brilliant season. In 1971 as a Dallas Cowboy, he scored the decisive touchdown in Super Bowl VI. As a head coach, he led the Chicago Bears to a near-perfect 17-1 season in 1985 and a decisive victory in Super Bowl XX. He was inducted into the Pro Football Hall of Fame in 1988.

"I'm not mean at all. I just try to protect myself. You'll see I don't ever pick on anybody who has a number above 30."

"I don't think anything is unrealistic if you believe you can do it."

"If you are determined enough and willing to pay the price, you can get it done."

Virginia Wade
Champion tennis player

"I always felt that I hadn't achieved what I wanted to achieve. I always felt I could get better. That's the whole incentive."

Mary Lou Retton
Gymnast, Olympic gold medalist

"I like added pressure. It makes me work harder."

Mary Decker
Distance runner

"I was born to be a runner. I simply love to run. It's almost like the faster I go, the easier it becomes."

Walter Camp
Football coach, Yale

"When it comes to the football field, mind will always win over muscle and brute force."

Branch Rickey
Major league baseball executive

"Problems are the price you pay for progress."

Joe Garagiola
Sports broadcaster

"Players have hurts and fears and anxieties. As an announcer, I'm strictly for the underdog."

Knute Rockne

1888 - 1931

A persuasive and charismatic leader, Knute Rockne understood the dynamics of motivation better than any man in the Golden Age of Sports. It was during a fiercely contested battle against Army in 1928 that he inspired his Notre Dame team to victory with the most romantic episode in the history of college football, the tale of a man named George Gipp, who got off a sick bed in the dead of winter to take the field one wind-blustered icy day—simply for the love of the game. "Win one for the Gipper" may be the most well-known rallying cry in sporting history. When Knute Rockne was killed in a plane crash in 1931, he had led his Fighting Irish to three consecutive national championships, posted a record of 105-12-5 and built a winning percentage, .881, that may never be surpassed.

"Football is a game played with the arms, legs, and shoulders—but mostly from the neck up."

"The secret of winning football games is working more as a team, less as individuals. I play not my 11 best, but my best 11."

"One man practicing sportsmanship is far better than a hundred teaching it."

Heywood Hale Broun
Writer

"Sports do not build character. They reveal it."

Stan Smith
Champion tennis player

"Experience tells you what to do; confidence allows you to do it."

Warren Spahn
Major league pitcher

"Hitting is timing. Pitching is upsetting timing."

Russell Baker
Writer

"In America, it is sport that is the opiate of the masses."

Lou Holtz
Football coach, University of Notre Dame

"If you burn your neighbor's house, it doesn't make your home look better."

Jack Benny
Comedian

"Give me golf clubs, fresh air and a beautiful partner, and you can keep my golf clubs and the fresh air."

Joe Paterno
Football coach, athletic director, Penn State

"Besides pride, loyalty, discipline, heart and mind, confidence is the key to all the locks."

Evelyn Ashford

1957 -

Blistering speed and a deep desire to win earned Evelyn Ashford a place on five consecutive Olympic teams. At a time when the East German women dominated the sprint, Ashford set her sights on regaining the gold for the United States. In addition to being an enormously talented runner, she was also a tireless worker, spending hour after hour sharpening her skills and improving her technique. Her no-nonsense, work-is-first method proved very effective, because when the time came for her to perform, she excelled. Ashford won four Olympic gold medals—the 100 meter in 1984, and the 4x100 meter in 1984, 1988 and 1982—as well as a silver medal in the 100 meter in 1988.

"I believe in women.
I believe in myself.
I believe in my body."

"Whatever muscles I have are the product of my own hard work— nothing else."

"I can feel the wind go by when I run. It feels good. It feels fast."

Fred Shero
NHL coach, general manager

"Experience is the name we give our mistakes."

Florence Griffith-Joyner
Sprinter, Olympic gold medalist

"Young people need positive role models. I would like to be one."

Steve McMichael
NFL tackle

"I think I'm going to be remembered as one of the craziest sons-of-guns who ever came down the pike, but I play the game with dignity."

Michelle McGann
LPGA golfer

"I was always my own person, not ever really trying to copy anybody."

Tommy Lasorda
Major league manager

"The only way I'd worry about the weather is if it snows on our side of the field and not theirs."

George Orwell
Writer

"Serious sport has nothing to do with fair play."

Arnold Palmer

1929 -

When he charged the fairways with his special brand of spirited enthusiasm, Arnold Palmer single-handedly awakened the American public to the world of golf. Though anything but a textbook player, his powerful stroke and determined focus captivated the imagination of men and women throughout the country. Palmer first made his presence known with a victory in the 1954 U.S. Amateur competition. Four years later, as a professional, he captured the first of his four Masters titles. Trailing by seven strokes at the start of the final round of play, he scored a miraculous come-from-behind victory by birdieing six of the first seven holes and shooting a 30 on the front nine. Palmer won 60 tournaments on the PGA Tour, including a victory at the Canadian PGA at the age of 51.

"I've always made a total effort, even when the odds seemed entirely against me."

"I play to win, everybody knows I play to win."

"I never quit trying. I never felt that I didn't have a chance to win."

Greg Norman
PGA golfer

"I'm a very intense person. When I go after something, I want to go after it with everything I have. I want to push myself to the edge."

Chuck Knox
NFL coach

"Practice without improvement is meaningless."

Roy Campanella
Major league catcher

"You gotta be a man to play baseball for a living, but you gotta have a lot of little boy in you, too."

Joe Paterno
Football coach, athletic director, Penn State

"Publicity is like poison. It doesn't hurt unless you swallow it."

Bob Hope
Comedian

"If you watch a game, it's fun. If you play it, it's recreation. If you work at it, it's golf."

Sebastian Coe
Distance runner, Olympic gold medalist

"All pressure is self-inflicted. It's what you make of it—or how you let it rub off on you."

Jack Nicklaus

1940 -

Jack Nicklaus is the most influential and arguably the finest golfer of all time. He captured the U.S. Open in 1962 and the Masters 24 years later, marking the longest stretch between first and last major titles in any sports career. With nearly 100 tour victories worldwide, including 20 major championships, his record is nothing short of astonishing. His victories include two U.S. Amateurs, four U.S. Opens, three British Opens, five PGA Championships and a record six Masters.

"The one strongest, most important idea in my game of golf—my cornerstone—is that I want to be the best. I wouldn't accept anything less than that. My ability to concentrate and work toward that goal has been my greatest asset."

"Through the years of experience I have found that air offers less resistance than dirt." [When asked why he tees up his ball so high.]

Evonne Goolagong
Champion tennis player

"When everybody said I'd never be any good again, it just made me push on."

Joe Robbie
Owner, Miami Dolphins

"There is no substitute for effort. Always play up to your full potential in every endeavor. The greatest extravagance of all is to waste human potential."

Chuck Mills
College football coach

"Some coaches pray for wisdom. I pray for 260-pound tackles."

David Feherty
PGA golfer

"It's how you deal with failure that determines how you achieve success."

Bill Bradley
U.S. Senator, NBA forward

"The taste of defeat has a richness of experience all its own."

Hubert Green
PGA golfer

"Winning breeds confidence, and confidence breeds winning."

Paul "Bear" Bryant

1913 - 1983

He began his coaching career at the University of Maryland in 1945, went on to Kentucky, then Texas A&M before settling in at Alabama. For the next quarter of a century, Bear Bryant coached the "Crimson Tide," guiding the likes of future professional quarterbacks Joe Namath, Ken Stabler and Richard Todd. He understood the importance of encouraging the individual while building the team. He led Alabama to five national championships and 15 bowl wins, including eight Sugar Bowls. When he died in 1983 at the age of 69, just four weeks after his last victory and six weeks after announcing his retirement, his 323-85-17 record made him the all-time winning coach in college football history.

"When you make a mistake, there are only three things you should ever do about it: 1. Admit it; 2. Learn from it, and, 3. Don't repeat it."

"Winning isn't everything, but it beats anything that comes in second."

"The competition in the job market today calls for being as well-prepared as possible. You must prepare for your future, and that key is education."

Nick Niccolau
NFL coach

"Our trainer has become so injury conscious that he is putting life jackets on the players before he allows them in the whirlpool."

Don Hutson
NFL offensive end

"For every pass I ever caught in a game, I caught a thousand in practice."

Billy Martin
Major league second baseman, manager

"When you're a winner, you come back no matter what happened the day before."

Bill Foster
NCAA basketball coach, Virginia Tech
"There's no letter 'I' in the word teamwork."

Mark Twain
Writer
"There is no use in your walking five miles to fish when you can depend on being as unsuccessful near home."

Tom Watson
PGA golfer
"I was not a winner when I first came out on the tour. I had to develop a trust in myself that I had the ability to win."

Nancy Lopez

1957 -

During her first full season on the Ladies Professional Golf Association Tour in 1978, Nancy Lopez won nine tournaments, including a record five in a row. She garnered Rookie of the Year honors for her exceptional play, collecting the Vare Trophy as well for the best tournament average, and was named *Golf Magazine* Player of the Year. Recognized for her consistency and power of concentration, Lopez became the dominant player on the LPGA Tour, establishing a new record low-stroke average at 70.73 in 1985. Today she remains one of the most popular players in the game, an outstanding star who reached the LPGA Hall of Fame by the age of 30.

"There has always been something new, demanding and testing every day I play. I love the challenge."

"The pressure makes me more intent about each shot."

"When I had to give up swimming because it wasn't good for my golfing muscles, I began to think of what else I would have to sacrifice if I wanted to keep playing golf."

Gale Sayers
NFL running back

"If you don't have enough pride, you're going to get your butt beat every play."

Mark Spitz
Swimmer, Olympic gold medalist

"I'm trying to do the best I can. I'm not concerned about tomorrow, but with what goes on today."

Lefty Gomez
Major league pitcher

"We lost 14 straight. Then we had a game rained out and it felt so good, we threw a victory dinner."

Howard Cosell
Sports broadcaster

"Sports is the toy department of human life."

Casey Stengel
Major league manager

"Managing is getting paid for home runs someone else hits."

Andre Agassi
Champion tennis player

"I've realized my dreams of winning a Grand Slam tournament. If my career was over tomorrow, I got more than I deserved, than I could ever ask for."

Joe DiMaggio
1914 -

A man of quiet grace and style, Joe DiMaggio made history in 1941 by hitting safely in 56 consecutive games, a sustained effort many experts consider the most remarkable achievement in all of sports. During a career interrupted for three years by World War II, DiMaggio hit 361 home runs, drove in 1,537 runs, posted one of the best-ever slugging percentages at .571 and compiled a .325 career batting average. He roamed the vast center field of Yankee Stadium with ease and confidence, and charged the base paths with speed and intelligence. In all, DiMaggio led the New York Yankees to 10 World Series titles in 13 seasons, leading the league in home runs, runs batted in, and batting average twice each. He was voted the league's Most Valuable Player three times.

"A person always doing his or her best becomes a natural leader, just by example."

"A ball player's got to be kept hungry to become a big leaguer. That's why no boy from a rich family ever made the big leagues."

"Live in hope and die in despair."

Don Carter
Champion bowler

"One of the advantages bowling has over golf is that you seldom lose a bowling ball."

Lawrence Taylor
NFL linebacker

"There are guys who want to shoot the last shot and others who want to pass off. I want that last shot."

Bob Devaney
Football coach, Nebraska

"I had a friend with a lifetime contract. After two bad years the university president called him into his office and pronounced him dead."

Nick Faldo
PGA golfer

"The word is control. That's my ultimate—to have control."

Julie Krone
Jockey

"With racing, you never rest on your laurels, and there are no counterfeits."

Samuel Johnson
Essayist, writer

"Angling—I can only compare to a stick and string, with a worm at one end and a fool at the other."

Earvin "Magic" Johnson
1959 -

A rare combination of size and speed, power and grace, Magic Johnson has been a marvel on the basketball court. As a freshman at Michigan State University, he led the Spartans to their first Big Ten championship in 19 years, as well as a National Collegiate Athletic Association title. In his rookie year in the National Basketball Association, he averaged 18 points, 10 rebounds, 10 assists and three steals per game, topping off the season with a stunning performance in the finals against the Philadelphia 76ers He was named the Playoff Most Valuable Player—the first rookie ever graced with the honor. In all, Magic garnered five NBA titles with the Lakers, three NBA All-Star MVPs, an NCAA championship and two Olympic gold medals.

"I've had a great life. I've lived a life that no one could have imagined for me or anyone else."

"I was given the gifts to become not only an athlete but also a businessman, a thinker who could help dispel the myth that most athletes are dumb jocks who can't see beyond the next game."

Lefty Gomez
Major league pitcher

"I'm throwing twice as hard as I used to, but the ball isn't going as fast."

Kareem Abdul-Jabbar
NBA center

"One man can be a crucial ingredient on a team, but one man cannot make a team."

Roger Staubach
NFL quarterback, sports broadcaster

"Confidence is the result of hours and days and weeks and years of constant work and dedication."

Leo Durocher
Major league manager

"How you play the game is for college boys. When you're playing for money, winning is the only thing that counts."

Bruce Jenner
Decathlete, Olympic gold medalist

"I learned that the only way you are going to get anywhere in life is to work hard at it. If you do, you'll win—if you don't, you won't."

Jack Roper
Heavyweight boxer

"I zigged when I should have zagged."

Joe Namath

1943 -

A brash and colorful competitor, Joe Namath led his New York Jets to the Super Bowl in 1969 in what appeared to be the mismatch of the century against the dominating Baltimore Colts. In some circles, the Colts were favored to win by as many as 45 points. Yet a week before the big showdown, Namath guaranteed victory—then went on to fulfill his promise with a brilliant performance against a surprised Baltimore team. For his heroic efforts, Namath was voted the Most Valuable Player of Super Bowl III. Voted twice to the all-AFL team, he was also voted all-NFL in 1972. He was elected to the Pro Football Hall of Fame in 1985.

"When you have confidence, you can have a lot of fun; and when you have fun, you can do amazing things."

"To be a leader, you have to make people want to follow you, and nobody wants to follow someone who doesn't know where he's going."

Miller Barber
PGA golfer

"I don't say my golf game is bad, but if I grew tomatoes, they'd come up sliced."

Wilt Chamberlain
NBA center

"If I can miss five minutes of one of his practices, I feel like I am adding five years to my life." [Discussing Coach Alex Hannum's training sessions.]

William Perry
NFL tackle

"When I was little, I was big."

Billy Tubbs
NCAA basketball coach, Texas Christian

"This year we plan to run and shoot. Next season we hope to run and score."

Fred Shero
NHL coach, general manager

"I'm like a duck: calm above water, but paddling like hell underneath."

Leo Durocher
Major league manager

"You don't save a pitcher for tomorrow. Tomorrow it may rain."

Lou Holtz

1937 -

As a young man, Lou Holtz was content to dream the dreams of small town life; his parents, however, dreamed bigger dreams for him, sending the lackluster student off to college. Little did anyone know that he was to become one of the most brilliant, motivational football coaches in the college ranks. After a brief stint coaching in the National Football League, he joined the University of Arkansas and was named National Coach of the Year in 1977 and Southwestern Conference Coach of the Year in 1979. Joining the University of Notre Dame in 1986, he led the Fighting Irish to an undefeated season and a national championship in 1988, rebuilding the reputation of the nation's most popular college team.

"I don't mind starting a season with unknowns. I just don't like finishing a season with a bunch of them."

"When all is said and done, as a rule, more is said than done."

"Coaching is nothing more than eliminating mistakes before you get fired."

Bill Vaughan
Writer

"As a nation we are dedicated to keeping physically fit—and parking as close to the stadium as possible."

Janet Evans
Swimmer, Olympic gold medalist

"On the starting block before my first Olympic race, I was smiling because I was having fun. That's what it is all about, to have fun."

Satchel Paige
Major league pitcher

"Don't look back. Someone might be gaining on you."

Theodore Roosevelt
24th president of the United States

"In life, as in a football game, the principle to follow is: Hit the line hard."

Buzzy Bavasi
Baseball executive

"We live by the Golden Rule. Those who have the gold make the rules."

Sam Snead
PGA golfer

"Forget your opponents; always play against par."

Wilma Rudolph
1940 - 1994

Miraculously, within four years of recovering from disabling bouts with pneumonia and scarlet fever, Wilma Rudolph became a superstar in both basketball and track, tying for first place in the 200-meter dash in the Olympic trials in 1956. After winning a bronze medal in the 400-meter relay in Melbourne that year—as well as the Sullivan Award, an honor given annually to America's outstanding athlete—Rudolph set her sights on the 1960 Olympics. There, in a stunning performance that made her the most celebrated Olympian in Rome, she won gold medals in the 400-meter relay and the 100 and 200-meter dashes—one of only three women to sweep the three sprint events.

"My mother taught me very early to believe I could achieve any accomplishment I wanted to. The first was to walk without braces."

"I would be very disappointed if I were only remembered as a runner because I feel that my contribution to the youth in America has far exceeded the woman who was the Olympic champion. The challenge is still there."

Peggy Fleming
Figure skater, Olympic gold medalist

"The most important thing is to love your sport. Never do it to please someone else. It has to be yours."

Dizzy Dean
Major league pitcher

"The Good Lord was good to me. He gave me a strong body, a good right arm and a weak mind."

JoAnne Carner
LPGA golfer

"Money was never a goal for me because of my amateur training. I was taught to win and that was it."

Joe Gibbs
NFL head coach

"People who enjoy what they are doing invariably do it well."

Reggie Jackson
Major league outfielder

"The will to win is worthless if you don't get paid for it."

Pop Warner
College football coach

"You play the way you practice."

Charles O. Finley
Owner, Oakland Athletics

"Sweat plus sacrifice equals success."

Bobby Hull

1939 -

Bobby Hull handled the puck with a precision that was both uncommon and unbelievable, with fairly incredible results: In 16 NHL seasons, he scored 610 goals and added 560 assists in regular-season games and produced another 62 goals and 67 assists in Stanley Cup play. He was the first player to score more than 50 goals in a season. He won the Art Ross Trophy, awarded annually to the league's leading scorer, three different times, the Hart Trophy as the NHL's Most Valuable Player, twice, and the Lady Bing Trophy, the symbol of large scoring numbers combined with sportsmanship. For his contributions to the game of hockey, Hull was awarded the Lester Patrick Trophy. He was voted to the All-Star team 12 times.

"Always keep your composure. You can't score from the penalty box; and to win, you have to score."

"Every professional athlete owes a debt of gratitude to the fans and management, and pays an installment every time he plays. He should never miss a payment."

Vin Scully
Sports broadcaster

"It's a mere moment in a man's life between an All-Star Game and an Old-Timers' Game."

Willie Shoemaker
Jockey

"I've always believed that anybody with a little ability, a little guts and the desire to apply himself can make it."

Joe Torre
Major league first baseman, manager

"I'm not sure whether I'd rather be managing or testing bulletproof vests."

Richard M. Nixon
37th president of the United States

"If I had my life to live all over again, I'd have ended up a sportswriter."

Julius Erving
NBA forward

"I keep both eyes on my man. The basket hasn't moved on me yet."

Sugar Ray Leonard
Boxer and sports broadcaster

"My ambition is not to be just a good fighter. I want to be great, something special."

Muhammad Ali

1942 -

With his flawless reflexes, punishing power and remarkable speed, Cassius Clay was destined to become one of the most celebrated professional fighters of all time. Making his championship debut in 1964, Clay, who made his first and last title fight under that name before changing it to Muhammad Ali according to Muslim custom, defeated Sonny Liston in a technical knock out. Over the next 15 years, Ali elevated the sport of boxing to new levels of popularity, becoming only the second man in history to recapture the heavyweight championship. Ali reigned for three more years before losing the title—only to regain it again seven months later for an unprecedented third time.

"You could be the world's best garbage man, the world's best model; it doesn't matter what you do if you're the best."

"There are no pleasures in a fight, but some of my fights have been a pleasure to win."

"Age is whatever you think it is. You are as old as you think you are."

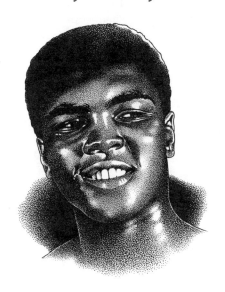

Joe Louis
Heavyweight boxer

"He can run, but he can't hide."

Steve Garvey
Major league first baseman

"You have to set the goals that are almost out of reach. If you set a goal that is attainable without much work or thought, you are stuck with something below your true talent and potential."

Pat Day
Jockey

"I know there's a Derby out there with my name on it."

Vernon Law
Major league pitcher

"Experience is a hard teacher because she gives the test first, the lesson afterwards."

Jerry Glanville
NFL head coach

"If you're a pro coach, NFL stands for Not For Long."

Erma Bombeck
Humorist

"If a man watches three football games in a row, he should be declared legally dead."

Michael Jordan

1963 -

When it came to grace and style on the basketball court, one player was truly in a league of his own. The skywalking, above-the-rim skills of Michael Jordan made him the dominating player in the National Basketball Association throughout his career—and the most recognized athlete in the world. His list of achievements is nothing short of breathtaking: College Player of the Year; three-time Olympic gold medalist; seven-time All-NBA 1st team; four-time regular season Most Valuable Player; four-time MVP of the NBA Finals; and NBA All-Star Game MVP.

"I've always tried to project everything positive. People say you need role models in the world, and people were asking for them, and I never thought a role model should be negative."

"Basketball is my escape, my refuge. It seems that everything else is so...so busy and complicated."

"The game is my wife. It demands loyalty and responsibility, and it gives me back fulfillment and peace."

Charlie Gehringer
Major league second baseman

"Ball players do things backward. First we play, then we retire and go to work."

Jack Thompson
NFL quarterback

"It's amazing what the human body can do when chased by a bigger human body."

Bonnie Blair
Speedskater, Olympic gold medalist

"My parents put skates on me at age 2, the way it should be if you're serious, and I've always liked it."

Leo Durocher
Major league manager

"Nice guys finish last."

Bud Wilkinson
NFL head coach

"You can motivate players better with kind words than you can with a whip."

Mario Andretti
Race car driver

"Desire is the key to motivation, but it's the determination and commitment to an unrelenting pursuit of your goal, a commitment to excellence, that will enable you to attain the success you seek."

John Wooden
1910 -

As a senior at Purdue University, John Wooden set a Big Ten scoring record, led Purdue to a national championship, and won College Player of the Year honors. After his days in the National Basketball Association, he settled in Los Angeles as head basketball coach with the University of California. There, throughout the 1960s and 70s, Wooden and his Bruins established a series of records that may never be broken: 88 consecutive victories; 10 National Collegiate Athletic Association titles, including seven consecutive crowns; 38 straight NCAA tournament victories and eight straight undefeated conference championships. Elected to the Basketball Hall of Fame as a player, Wooden was also so honored as a coach—the only man to be recognized in both fields.

"Class is an intangible quality which commands, rather than demands, the respect of others."

"It's not so important who starts the game, but who finishes it."

"It's what you learn after you know it all that counts."

Bo Jackson
NFL running back, major league outfielder

"I'll never worry about not being successful. I'll just take it one day at a time and play the best I can."

Lefty Gomez
Major league pitcher

"The secret of my success is clean living and a fast outfield."

Damon Runyon
Writer

"The race is not always to the swift nor the battle to the strong—but that's the way to bet it."

Bob Cousy
NBA guard

"Michael Jordan goes up, stops for a cup of coffee, looks over the scenery, then follows through with a tomahawk jam."

Rick Mears
Race car driver

"There's nothing quite like Pole Day at Indy. The pressure is so intense. You have to do four perfect laps. The race is a piece of cake by comparison: You have 500 miles to get it right."

Walter Payton

1954 -

He was called "Sweetness," but Walter Payton was one of the most determined, dominating and successful running backs in the history of the National Football League. He carried the ball more times for more yards than any other player. Over the course of his 13-year career, he set a string of records that is staggering: most seasons rushing over 1,000 yards (10); most yards in a single game (275); receptions by a running back (486); consecutive seasons with 1,000 yards or more (6); most yards carried (16,726); and consecutive seasons leading the league in rushing (4). In 1985, Payton and the Chicago Bears were practically unbeatable; only a loss to the Miami Dolphins marred a perfect season, a season that culminated with a resounding 46-10 victory over the New England Patriots in Super Bowl XX.

"I'll take a game-winning 1-yard plunge over a futile 90-yard breakaway any day."

95

"I want to be remembered as the guy who gave his all whenever he was on the field. I want people to know that Walter Payton will be putting out on every play."

Walter
Payton
1954 –

He
was
called "but
Walter Payton was one
determined,
and successful running

Yogi Berra
Major league catcher, manager

"So I'm ugly. So what? I never saw anyone hit with his face."

Bo Jackson
NFL running back, major league outfielder

"If my doctor says I can play, believe me, you'll see me out there getting the guts kicked out of me, or me kicking the guts out of somebody else."

Gary Player
PGA golfer

"If I had to choose between my wife and my putter, well, I'd miss her."

Brian Bosworth
NFL linebacker

"If you can miss getting up in the morning and running into a wall, I miss playing football."

Cal Ripken Jr.
Major league shortstop

"I never perceived myself to be the big star. I'm only one of nine guys. I think it is good to think that way."

Casey Stengel
Major league manager

"I was not successful as a ball player, as it was a game of skill."

Mildred "Babe" Didrikson Zaharias

1914 - 1956

A tall and slender woman of enormous ability, Mildred "Babe" Didrikson Zaharias is considered the greatest female athlete of all time. She dominated women's sports in America for more than a quarter of a century with an overwhelming combination of raw power, agility and natural talent. She was an accomplished baseball player, a world-class diver, swimmer, an Olympic silver medalist in the high jump and a gold medalist in the javelin and 80-meter low hurdles. She helped found the Ladies' Professional Golf Association after winning 17 consecutive amateur tournaments and went on to dominate the LPGA Tour by winning 10 major championships, including three U.S. Open championships and four Western Opens. She was chosen "Athlete of the Half Century" by the Associated Press in 1950.

"As long as I am improving, I will go on."

"All of my life I've been competing and competing to win."

"I don't seem able to do my best unless I'm behind or in trouble."

Maureen Connolly
Champion tennis player

"Tennis can be a grind, and there is always the danger of going stale if you think about it too much. You have to be able to relax between matches and tournaments."

Rodney Dangerfield
Comedian

"I went to a fight the other night, and a hockey game broke out."

Eric Dickerson
NFL running back

"If I've lost a step, it's a step a lot of other guys never had."

Roger Maris
Major league outfielder

"I'll never take abuse from anybody, big or small, important or unimportant, if I think it's undeserved."

Isiah Thomas
NBA guard

"If all I'm remembered for is being a good basketball player, then I've done a bad job with the rest of my life."

Bryant Gumbel
Sports broadcaster, former Today Show *host*

"The other sports are just sports. Baseball is a love."

Lee Trevino

1939 -

When he defeated the legendary Jack Nicklaus by four strokes at the U.S. Open at Oak Hill in 1968, Lee Trevino captured the attention of the golfing world with his unorthodox character and entertaining style. But although the stars did not always approve of his nonstop jokes and running chatter, they respected his magical skills on the fairways and his brilliant golf-course strategy—as well as his uncanny ability to bring in the spectators. During his professional career, Trevino was a two-time winner of three major championships—the U.S. Open, the British Open and the PGA. After 27 victories on the PGA Tour, he went on to become one of the leading celebrities on the U.S. Senior Tour. PGA Player of the Year in 1971, he entered the World Golf Hall of Fame in 1981.

"There's no such thing as natural touch. Touch is something you create by hitting millions of golf balls."

"If you are caught on a golf course during a storm and are afraid of lightning, hold up a one-iron. Not even God can hit a one-iron."

Tommy Lasorda
Major league manager

"Managing is like holding a dove in your hand. Squeeze too hard and you kill it, not hard enough and it flies away."

Bobby Nichols
PGA golfer

"If you've got to remind yourself to concentrate during competition, you've got no chance to concentrate."

Stirling Moss
Race car driver

"To achieve anything in this game, you must be prepared to dabble on the boundary of disaster."

Jackie Robinson
Major league second baseman

"Many people resented my impatience and honesty, but I never cared about acceptance as much as I cared about respect."

Bo Jackson
NFL running back, major league outfielder

"Regardless of whether I hit a 440-foot home run or strike out, the game will always be fun. All I want is to be able to get in some quality cuts every at-bat."

Mickey Mantle
1931 - 1995

Mickey Mantle was the most feared hitter in baseball, a devastating player who could hit tape-measure home runs from either side of the plate. Replacing the legendary Joe DiMaggio in 1952, his nearly limitless talents led the New York Yankees to 12 fall classics in 14 years, including seven World Championships. He established World Series records for most home runs, runs batted in, runs and bases on balls. In 1956, one of his finest seasons, Mantle hit 52 home runs with 130 RBIs and a .353 batting average to win the Triple Crown. He also led the league with 132 runs, a .705 slugging percentage and 112 walks, capping the year with the first of his three Most Valuable Player awards.

"I'd go back to making $100,000 a year in a second if I could play ball again."

"To play ball was all I lived for."

"During my 18 years I came to bat almost 109,000 times. I struck out about 1,700 times and walked maybe 1,800 times. You figure a ballplayer will average about 500 at-bats a season. That means I played seven years in the major leagues without even hitting the ball."

Paul O'Neil
Writer

"The art of running the mile consists in essence of reaching the threshold of unconsciousness at the instant of breasting the tape."

Paul Brown
NFL coach

"A winner never whines."

Tommy Lasorda
Major league manager

"I've learned that the only way to get respect from people is to give them respect—and that's my way of doing it."

Joe Louis
Heavyweight boxer

"Every man's got to figure to get beat sometime."

Scottie Pippen
NBA forward

"I've always led by example, and I'm not that vocal."

Baron Pierre de Coubertin
Founder, Modern Olympic Games

"The important thing in the Olympic Games is not to win but to take part; the important thing in life is not the triumph but the struggle. The essential thing is not to have conquered but to have fought well."

Joe Montana

1956 -

After leading the University of Notre Dame to the national title in 1977, Joe Montana was drafted by the San Francisco 49ers, a team that had never been to a Super Bowl. By the close of the season in 1989, they had played in four Super Bowls—and had won them all. Considered by many to be the finest quarterback in the history of the National Football League, Montana dissected defenses with surgeon-like precision. Ranked in the top 10 in all-time passing efficiency, yards passing and touchdown passes, he earned back-to-back regular season Most Valuable Player honors in 1989 and 1990. Even more remarkable, he is the only three-time Super Bowl MVP in the history of the NFL.

"Confidence is a very fragile thing. Just because you have it in college doesn't mean you're gonna have it in the pros."

"Me, a Notre Dame legend? I go to the store, buy milk and forget the bread. I try to hammer a nail and hit my thumb. Do legends do that?"

Ben Crenshaw
PGA golfer

"Golf is the hardest game in the world. There's no way you can ever get it. Just when you think you do, the game jumps up and puts you in your place."

Roger Bannister
Distance runner

"Without the concentration of the mind and the will, performance would not result."

Bum Phillips
NFL head coach

"The only discipline that lasts is self-discipline."

Max Baer
Heavyweight boxer

"If you ever get belted and see three fighters through a haze, go after the one in the middle. That's what ruined me—I went after the two guys on the end."

John Bach
NBA coach

"Defense starts with a determination and pride to excel. It comes with knowledge and communication, and you've got to have heart. To the timid soul, nothing is possible. To the aggressor, everything is possible."

Jimmy Connors
1952 -

For more than two decades, the seemingly ageless Jimmy Connors sent his two-fisted backhand roaring across the net with startling precision. His powerful baseline style earned him the number-one ranking in the world for five consecutive years. Considered feisty and controversial in his early days on the circuit, he became the grand old man of tennis, earning the respect and admiration of both the public and the media. In all, Connors was ranked in the U.S. Top Ten a record 20 times during his 21-year professional career. He was the all-time leader in professional singles titles and matches won at both the U.S. Open and Wimbledon.

"I don't want to hear about number two. There's only one number one. It's not a matter of money—just pride—pure and simple. I want to be the best."

"I hate to lose more than I like to win. I hate to see the happiness on their faces when they beat me."

"The problem is that when you get experience, you're too damned old to do anything about it."

Emory Jones
St. Louis Blues Arena manager

"Hockey players are like mules. They have no fear of punishment and no hope of reward."

Roger Maris
Major league outfielder

"I do know that when I'm not hitting, my wife could pitch and get me out."

Virginia Wade
Champion tennis player

"Winners aren't popular. Losers often are."

John Brodie
NFL quarterback

"There is an intensity and a danger in football—as in life generally—which keeps us alive and awake. It is a test of our awareness and ability. Like so much of life, it presents us with the choice of responding either with fear or with action."

Sugar Ray Robinson
Middleweight boxer

"Boxing is the art of self-defense. You have to pattern your style for each fight against the style of the man you're fighting."

Vince Lombardi
1913 - 1970

When Vince Lombardi accepted the head coaching position at Green Bay, he inherited a team of aging veterans and fresh rookies—and created one of the most dominating teams in National Football League history. He was strict but fair, and he accepted nothing less than the absolute best from his players. And they responded. His motivational techniques have been heralded for generating success inside and outside the world of sports. Among NFL coaches, his winning percentage of 74 percent remains an unparalleled standard. In a seven-year span, his Packers won five NFL championships, providing dominating victories in the first two Super Bowls.

"Coaches who can outline plays on a blackboard are a dime a dozen. The ones who win get inside their players and motivate."

"If you aren't fired with enthusiasm, you will be fired with enthusiasm."

"Winning isn't everything, but making the effort to win is."

Casey Stengel
Major league manager

"I'll say this. This is the greatest ball club a man could manage. Certainly the best I've ever known. I am indebted to them for the way they came through for me. They won it, not me." [Reflecting on the New York Yankees.]

Matt Biondi
Swimmer, Olympic gold medalist

"There is too much emphasis on success and failure, and too little on how a person grows as he works. Enjoy the journey, enjoy every moment, and quit worrying about winning and losing."

Bruce Jenner
Decathlete, Olympic gold medalist

"An athlete has such a narrow view of life he does not know reality."

Mario Andretti
Race car driver

"Circumstances may cause interruptions and delays, but never lose sight of your goal. Prepare yourself in every way you can by increasing your knowledge and adding to your experience, so that you can make the most of opportunity when it occurs."

Martina Navratilova

1956 -

In 1978, at the age of 21, Martina Navratilova captured her first title at Wimbledon. Days later, she was ranked the top player in women's tennis for the first time as well. With a blistering serve and a rock-solid groundstroke, the left-handed Navratilova would emerge as the dominant player in women's tennis throughout the last half of the 1980s. She captured her record ninth Wimbledon title in 1990, and at one point won 74 consecutive matches over 11 months and 13 tournaments. In all, Navratilova has won 18 Grand Slam singles titles—including six straight—and 37 Grand Slam doubles titles. She is the all-time women's leader in singles titles and money won.

"You have to want to win and expect that you are going to win. Top players have that edge."

"I just try to concentrate on concentrating."

"I hope, when I stop, people will think that somehow I mattered."

POWERFUL INSIGHTS TO IMPROVE
YOUR CAREER, YOUR BUSINESS, YOUR LIFE.

Successories, Inc. 1-800-535-2773